# Southern

AMERICAN

REGIONAL COOKING
LIBRARY
Culture, Tradition,
and History

*African American*

*American Indian*

*Amish and Mennonite*

*California*

*Hawaiian*

*Louisiana*

*Mexican American*

*Mid-Atlantic*

*Midwest*

*New England*

*Northwest*

*Southern Appalachia*

*Southern*

*Texas*

*Thanksgiving*

# Southern

Mason Crest Publishers

Philadelphia

Mason Crest Publishers Inc.
370 Reed Road
Broomall, Pennsylvania 19008
(866) MCP-BOOK (toll free)
www.masoncrest.com

First printing
1 2 3 4 5 6 7 8 9 10

Library of Congress Cataloging-in-Publication Data

Libal, Joyce.
  Southern.
      p. cm. — (American regional cooking library)
  Includes bibliographical references and index.
  ISBN 1-59084-621-4
  1. Cookery, American—Southern style—Juvenile literature.  I. Title. II. Series.
  TX715.2.S68L5197 2004
  641.5975—dc22

2004013340

Recipes contributed by Patricia Therrien.
Recipes tested and prepared by Bonni Phelps.
Produced by Harding House Publishing Services, Inc., Vestal, New York.
Interior design by Dianne Hodack.
Cover design by Michelle Bouch.
Printed and bound in the Hashemite Kingdom of Jordan.

# Contents

# *Introduction*
## by the Culinary Institute of America

Cooking is a dynamic profession, one that presents some of the greatest challenges and offers some of the greatest rewards. Since 1946, the Culinary Institute of America has provided aspiring and seasoned food service professionals with the knowledge and skills needed to become leaders and innovators in this industry.

Here at the CIA, we teach our students the fundamental culinary techniques they need to build a sound foundation for their food service careers. There is always another level of perfection for them to achieve and another skill to master. Our rigorous curriculum provides them with a springboard to continued growth and success.

Food is far more than simply sustenance or the source of energy to fuel you and your family through life's daily regimen. It conjures memories throughout life, summoning up the smell, taste, and flavor of simpler times. Cooking is more than an art and a science; it provides family history. Food prepared with care epitomizes the love, devotion, and culinary delights that you offer to your friends and family.

A cuisine provides a way to express and establish customs—the way a food should taste and the flavors and aromas associated with that food. Cuisines are more than just a collection of ingredients, cooking utensils, and dishes from a geographic location; they are elements that are critical to establishing a culinary identity.

When you can accurately read a recipe, you can trace a variety of influences by observing which ingredients are selected and also by noting the technique that is used. If you research the historical origins of a recipe, you may find ingredients that traveled from East to West or from the New World to the Old. Traditional methods of cooking a dish may have changed with the times or to meet special challenges.

The history of cooking illustrates the significance of innovation and the trading or sharing of ingredients and tools between societies. Although the various cooking vessels over the years have changed, the basic cooking methods have remained the same. Through adaptation, a recipe created years ago in a remote corner of the world could today be recognized by many throughout the globe.

When observing the customs of different societies, it becomes apparent that food brings people together. It is the common thread that we share and that we value. Regardless of the occasion, food is present to celebrate and to comfort. Through food we can experience other cultures and lands, learning the significance of particular ingredients and cooking techniques.

As you begin your journey through the culinary arts, keep in mind the power that food and cuisine holds. When passed from generation to generation, family heritage and traditions remain strong. Become familiar with the dishes your family has enjoyed through the years and play a role in keeping them alive. Don't be afraid to embellish recipes along the way – creativity is what cooking is all about.

# *Southern Culture, History, and Traditions*

Long ago, only Native tribes lived along the southeastern lands of North America. Beginning in the 1600s, though, a mix of immigrants came to live in the area that would be North Carolina, South Carolina, Georgia, and Florida.

Settlers from England, Scotland, Ireland, France, Spain, Germany, Asia, and the Netherlands have all influenced the culture and food traditions of these states, and American Indians' influence has continued to be strong as well. One of the most critical things that shaped the development of Southern culture and cuisine, however, was the two centuries of slave trade that forced people from West Africa to American shores. Thousands of Africans were made to work as slaves on Southern plantations. Here, creative African women skillfully combined knowledge of foods grown on the African continent with ingredients they found in Southern kitchens to develop a rich cuisine that lives to this day.

The tough times that followed the Civil War were just as responsible for the development of Southern cuisine as the prosperous economy of the South prior to the war. African cooks and other Southern women were as adept at making the simplest foods delicious as they were at incorporating a wealth of available ingredients into elegant dishes. From poke salad (made from a wild green) to hoecakes (a simple cornmeal pancake originally cooked over a fire on the blade of a hoe), to delicate seafood combinations, Southern cooking has withstood the test of time and economic hardship to emerge as one of the great national cuisines.

# Before you cook...

If you haven't done much cooking before, you may find recipe books a little confusing. Certain words and terms can seem unfamiliar. You may find the measurements difficult to understand. What appears to be an easy or familiar dish may contain ingredients you've never heard of before. You might not understand what utensil the recipe calls for you to use, or you might not be sure what the recipe is asking you to do.

Reading the pages in this section before you get started may help you understand the directions better so that your cooking goes more smoothly. You can also refer back to these pages whenever you run into questions.

## Safety Tips

Cooking involves handling very hot and very sharp objects, so being careful is common sense. What's more, you want to be certain that anything you plan on putting in your mouth is safe to eat. If you follow these easy tips, you should find that cooking can be both fun and safe.

# Before you cook...

- Always wash your hands before and after handling food. This is particularly important after you handle raw meats, poultry, and eggs, as bacteria called salmonella can live on these uncooked foods. You can't see or smell salmonella, but these germs can make you or anyone who swallows them very sick.
- Make a habit of using potholders or oven mitts whenever you handle pots and pans from the oven or microwave.
- Always set pots, pans, and knives with their handles away from counter edges. This way you won't risk catching your sleeves on them—and any younger children in the house won't be in danger of grabbing something hot or sharp.
- Don't leave perishable food sitting out of the refrigerator for more than an hour or two.
- Wash all raw fruits and vegetables to remove dirt and chemicals.
- Use a cutting board when chopping vegetables or fruit, and always cut away from yourself.
- Don't overheat grease or oil—but if grease or oil does catch fire, don't try to extinguish the flames with water. Instead, throw baking soda or salt on the fire to put it out. Turn all stove burners off.
- If you burn yourself, immediately put the burn under cold water, as this will prevent the burn from becoming more painful.
- Never put metal dishes or utensils in the microwave. Use only microwave-proof dishes.
- Wash cutting boards and knives thoroughly after cutting meat, fish or poultry — especially when raw and before using the same tools to prepare other foods such as vegetables and cheese. This will prevent the spread of bacteria such as salmonella.
- Keep your hands away from any moving parts of appliances, such as mixers.
- Unplug any appliance, such as a mixer, blender, or food processor before assembling for use or disassembling after use.

# Metric Conversion Table

Most cooks in the United States use measuring containers based on an eight-ounce cup, a teaspoon, and a tablespoon. Meanwhile, cooks in Canada and Europe are more apt to use metric measurements. The recipes in this book use cups, teaspoons, and tablespoons—but you can convert these measurements to metric by using the table below.

Temperature
To convert Fahrenheit degrees to Celsius, subtract 32 and multiply by .56.

212ºF = 100ºC
(this is the boiling point of water)
250ºF = 110ºC
275ºF = 135ºC
300ºF = 150ºC
325ºF = 160ºC
350ºF = 180ºC
375ºF = 190ºC
400ºF = 200ºC

Liquid Measurements
1 teaspoon = 5 milliliters
1 tablespoon = 15 milliliters
1 fluid ounce = 30 milliliters
1 cup = 240 milliliters
1 pint = 480 milliliters
1 quart = 0.95 liters
1 gallon = 3.8 liters

Measurements of Mass or Weight
1 ounce = 28 grams
8 ounces = 227 grams
1 pound (16 ounces) = 0.45 kilograms
2.2 pounds = 1 kilogram

Measurements of Length
¼ inch = 0.6 centimeters
½ inch = 1.25 centimeters
1 inch = 2.5 centimeters

# Pan Sizes

Baking pans are usually made in standard sizes. The pans used in the United States are roughly equivalent to the following metric pans:

9-inch cake pan = 23-centimeter pan
11x7-inch baking pan = 28x18-centimeter baking pan
13x9-inch baking pan = 32.5x23-centimeter baking pan
9x5-inch loaf pan = 23x13-centimeter loaf pan
2-quart casserole = 2-liter casserole

# Useful Tools, Utensils, Dishes

baking sheet

biscuit cutter

blender

breadboard

cheese shredder

electric mixer

food processor

garlic press

loaf pan     nut chopper     pastry blender     rice cooker

rolling pin     slow cooker     mallet

# *Cooking Glossary*

*cream* Combine butter or shortening with sugar until mixture is smooth and creamy.

*cut* Mix solid shortening or butter into flour, usually by using a pastry blender or two knives and making short, chopping strokes until the mixture looks like small pellets.

*dash* A very small amount.

*diced* Cut into small cubes or pieces.

*dollop* A small mound, about 1 or 2 tablespoons.

*fold* Gently combine a lighter substance with a heavier batter by spooning the lighter mixture through the heavier one without using strong beating strokes.

*julienned* Cut into small, thin strips.

*knead* To work dough with the hands, lifting the far edge, placing it upon the rest, and pushing with the heal of the hands.

*minced* Cut into very small pieces.

*seeded* With seeds removed.

*set* When a food preparation has completed the thickening process and can be sliced.

*simmer* Gently boiling, so that the surface of the liquid just ripples.

*toss* Turn food over quickly and lightly so that it is evenly covered with a liquid or powder.

*whisk* Stir briskly with a wire whisk.

*zest* A piece of the peel of lemon, lime, or orange that has been grated.

# *Special Southern Flavors*

cinnamon

cornmeal

limes

molasses

nutmeg

peaches

pecans

Vidalia onions

vinegar

# Southern Recipes

# Scotch Eggs

*The portability of this food has made it popular among Southern fishermen and hunters. You'll find the make-ahead food perfect for picnics or even busy mornings when you need to eat breakfast on the run.*

**Preheat oven to 350° Fahrenheit.**

## Ingredients:

*4 eggs, hard-boiled and peeled (see "Tip")*
*1 pound bulk pork sausage*
*1 tablespoon grated onion*
*1 tablespoon chopped parsley*
*¼ teaspoon cinnamon*
*⅛ teaspoon nutmeg*
*½ cup dry bread crumbs*

*Cooking utensils you'll need:*
*measuring spoons*
*grater*
*mixing bowl*
*baking dish*

## Directions:

Mix sausage with onion. Stir in parsley, cinnamon, and nutmeg, and divide mixture into 4 equal-sized piles. Use your hands to mold each pile around a hard-boiled egg, then roll them in the bread crumbs, place them in the baking dish, and bake until nicely browned (usually about 15 to 20 minutes).

## Tip:

To hard boil eggs, place them in a saucepan, cover with cold water, bring to boil over medium heat, lower heat, and boil gently for 5 minutes. To make them easier to peel, drain eggs and cover them with cold water until cool enough to handle. Roll each egg on a hard surface to crack shells before peeling.

## Southern History

In colonial times, many Scotch immigrants were pulled to America by the promise of land ownership. These people were often educated, skilled workers. Even those who paid for their voyage across the Atlantic by becoming indentured servants were well equipped to lead successful, independent lives when their period of work expired. They were thrifty, hardworking people, who brought with them customs and traditions—and their recipes.

At first, many of the Scotch settled in the middle colonies, especially in Pennsylvania where the city of Philadelphia was a major port where immigrants landed. Over subsequent years, however, the Scotch migrated south following the Great Philadelphia Road, the main route used for settling the interior southern colonies. Traveling down Virginia's Shenandoah Valley, then south into the North Carolina Piedmont region, they reached South Carolina by the 1760s. Settlers here often became frontiersmen and Indian fighters. Presidents Andrew Jackson and Ronald Reagan traced their roots to these early Americans.

# Southern Peach Bread

*Preheat oven to 325° Fahrenheit.*

## Ingredients:

½ cup shortening
½ cup sugar
2 eggs
2¼ cups pureed peaches (see "Tips")
1 teaspoon baking soda
1 teaspoon baking powder
¼ teaspoon salt
1 teaspoon cinnamon
1 teaspoon vanilla
2 cups flour
1 cup chopped pecans

*Cooking utensils you'll need:*
*blender or food processor*
*measuring cups*
*measuring spoons*
*nut chopper*
*mixing bowl*
*2 loaf pans*

## Directions:

Grease and lightly flour loaf pans and set them aside. *Cream* shortening with sugar, and stir in eggs one at a time. Stir in remaining ingredients in the order listed, divide mixture between the loaf pans, and bake for 55 to 60 minutes. Cool bread in pans for 5 minutes, then remove from pans to complete cooling.

## Tips:

Peel peaches, remove pits, and cut them into large chunks. Canned peaches can be substituted. Place chunks in blender container or food processor and process just until smooth.

Unless instructed to do otherwise in a recipe, always use large eggs when baking.

## Southern Food History

Colonists first began growing peaches in Georgia during the 1700s. New varieties were developed after the Civil War, making commercial production more successful. Among the new varieties was a larger, better-colored peach called Elberta. Today, more than forty varieties are grown commercially in Georgia, yet the state is actually third in peach production behind California and Georgia's southern neighbor, South Carolina. Fresh Southern peaches are only available for about sixteen weeks annually. Watch for them in your supermarket from May through August.

# Beaten Biscuits

*Before baking powder and baking soda became available, good old "elbow grease" was sometimes used to beat air into a batter. That's the case with these traditional Southern biscuits that are folded and pounded repeatedly to add air to the dough.*

**Preheat oven to 400° Fahrenheit.**

## Ingredients:

4 cups flour
1 teaspoon salt
¼ cup vegetable shortening
(Old-time Southern cooks would have used lard.)
2 tablespoons butter, softened
1 cup cold milk

*Cooking utensils you'll need:*
*measuring cups*
*measuring spoons*
*mixing bowl*
*pastry blender (optional)*
*breadboard (or other flat surface)*
*wooden mallet*
*rolling pin*
*biscuit cutter (or round glass)*
*baking sheet*

## Directions:

Grease baking sheet lightly and set it aside. Mix flour with salt. Use your hands to mix in the shortening and butter. (An alternative is to *cut* in shortening and butter with a pastry blender.) Make a depression in the center of the mixture, pour in the milk, and stir. Place the dough on a lightly floured breadboard or other flat surface and *knead* it a couple of times. Then push the dough down until it is only 1-inch thick, take the wooden mallet or similar wooden tool, and beat the dough. After you have hit the entire surface, fold dough in half and beat it again. Continue doing this for 20 or 30 minutes. Roll dough about ½-inch thick. Use a biscuit cutter or glass dipped in flour to cut biscuits, place them on the prepared baking sheet, prick each biscuit a couple of times with a fork, and bake until nicely browned (usually about 20 to 25 minutes). Serve biscuits hot with butter.

## *Tip:*

If you'd like to make biscuits but don't have time to beat the dough, add 4 teaspoons of baking powder to the recipe.

### *Southern Food History*

The word "biscuit" comes from the Latin word *bis coctum*, which means "twice baked." According to an early historical record, biscuits date all the way back to second-century Rome. Biscuits then were unleavened, hard, thin wafers. Since they contained very little moisture, they were ideal for storing, as they didn't become moldy very easily. As people started to explore the globe, biscuits (often called hardtack) became the ideal traveling food, because they stayed fresh for long periods. For centuries, biscuits were on board any ship that went to sea. These iron-like crackers could last for months, and even years under the right conditions. During the early settlement of North America, the Revolutionary War, and on through the Civil War, armies were kept alive with hardtack.

During the Civil War, soldiers in both the Northern and Southern armies were usually issued one half pound of beans or peas, bacon, pickled beef, compressed mixed vegetables—and one pound of hardtack. These biscuits were so hard they were often broken with a rock or rifle butt, and then sucked on until they were soft enough to be chewed and swallowed. Other times, the hardtack was soaked in water and then fried in bacon grease. Soldiers called the biscuits "sheet iron crackers" and "teeth dullers."

## Southern Food History

Vidalia onions are available for about nine months each year. With a sugar content that rivals that of apples, Vidalia onions add a sweet onion flavor to soups, stews, salads, and sandwiches. This is a newer vegetable, having been developed by happy accident in 1931. Even though this was the time of the Great Depression, these first onions were so tasty people were willing to pay $3.50 for a fifty-pound bag. Within ten years, the onions were being sold at a well-known farmer's market in Vidalia, Georgia. Word of the sweet onions continued to spread, and by the 1970s, this special vegetable could be purchased in many grocery stores. Since then, production and distribution have continued to grow, so much so that in 1990 it was named the state vegetable of Georgia. Today, about $50 million of the state's annual economy comes from sales of Vidalia onions. No wonder annual festivals are held each year in Vidalia and Glennville, Georgia, to honor and promote Vidalia onions.

# Vidalia Onion and Ham Bruschetta

*The South is famous for mouth-watering ham. Here it is combined with Georgia's sweet Vidalia onions to make a sophisticated Italian dish that's perfect for brunch or lunch.*

**Preheat oven to 400° Fahrenheit.**

## Ingredients:

4 ounces cooked ham, cut into 1–inch pieces (¾ cup)
1 cup chopped Vidalia onions
1 cup chopped plum tomatoes
2 tablespoons mayonnaise
1 tablespoon Dijon mustard
8 thick slices of Italian bread

*Cooking utensils you'll need:*
measuring cups
measuring spoon
mixing bowl
small bowl
baking sheet

## Directions:

Mix ham with onions and tomatoes and set aside. Mix mayonnaise with mustard in small bowl. Stir mayonnaise mixture into ham mixture. Place bread on baking sheet, divide ham mixture among bread slices, and bake for 10 to 15 minutes. Serve hot or cooled.

## Tip:

To reduce the calories in this dish, use low-fat ham and reduced-calorie mayonnaise.

# She-Crab Soup

*This creamy soup is a favorite in Charleston, South Carolina.*

## Ingredients:

1 tablespoon butter
1 tablespoon flour
1 quart milk
⅛ teaspoon mace
⅛ teaspoon pepper
1 teaspoon salt
½ teaspoon Worcestershire sauce
2 cups white crabmeat with roe (see "Tips")
6 tablespoons cooking sherry
½ cup heavy cream (whipping cream)
1 tablespoon chopped fresh parsley

*Cooking utensils you'll need:*
*measuring cups*
*measuring spoons*
*double boiler*
*small saucepan*
*electric mixer*
*mixing bowl*

## Directions:

Half fill the bottom of the double boiler with water, place it over medium heat, and bring to a gentle boil. Place butter in top portion of double boiler, and place over the hot water. When butter has melted, stir in flour. Slowly stir in milk, mace, pepper, salt, and Worcestershire sauce, and cook, stirring constantly, until smooth. Add crabmeat and roe, and cook for an additional 20 minutes. Meanwhile, put sherry in the small saucepan, place over medium heat, boil for about 30 seconds to remove alcohol, and set aside. Whip cream taking care not to over whip. To serve soup, place 1 tablespoon of sherry in each serving bowl, ladle soup on top of sherry, add a *dollop* of cream and a *dash* of parsley.

## Tips:

Mace comes from the red outer covering of the nutmeg seed. If you do not have mace in your kitchen, use nutmeg as a substitute.

Roe is another word for the eggs of fish or shellfish. If you cannot find crab roe, crumbled yolks from hard-boiled eggs are a good substitute. (To hard boil eggs, see "Tip" on page 18.)

## Southern Food Tradition

She-crab soup has long been associated with Charleston. According to tradition, it was first created by a butler in the home of one of Charleston's wealthiest families, the Rhetts. The original soup contained twelve crabs and only one teaspoon of flour. A puree of rice cooked in milk was used to thicken the broth.

Today, the state of South Carolina protects its crabs by enforcing two specific laws about catching them. First, whether you are an individual crabbing on the beach or a commercial crabber with crab pots, and whether the crab is male or female, it must measure five inches across the top or be released. In the winter, the female crabs have their roe—tiny, orange eggs that give a delicate color and flavor to genuine she-crab soup. According to the second law, if the eggs are showing outside the female crab's shell, you must release the crab regardless of its size. Females with roe inside that is not visible provide enough roe to keep she-crab soup-lovers happy.

Many recipes specify she-crabs, so if you want your soup to be the real thing, you need to be able to tell females from males. Luckily, this is easy to do, and you won't need a magnifying glass. Simply look at the underside of the crab. The female has a broad, triangle-shaped area in the center of the shell, while the male has a long, thin spire-shape.

## Southern History

On a mid-December day in 1903, the crabs that scuttled along North Carolina's Outer Banks were disturbed by a strange shadow passing overhead. Little did they know that human life had been forever altered by Orville and Wilbur Wright. The Wright brothers selected Kitty Hawk for the first flight of their "heavier-than-air machine" because of the favorable high winds that blew dependably in the area. The enormous sand dunes, inhabited only by crabs and other wildlife, also made the area attractive for the experimental flight of the first successful aircraft.

# Crab Dip

## Ingredients:

1 cup mayonnaise
1 (10 ½-ounce) can cream of mushroom soup
½ cup **minced** onions
1 cup shredded cheddar cheese
½ teaspoon salt
¼ teaspoon pepper
1 pound white crabmeat
crackers

**Cooking utensils you'll need:**
measuring cups
measuring spoons
cheese shredder
slow cooker

## Directions:

Mix mayonnaise and soup in slow cooker. Stir in onions, cheese, salt, and pepper. *Fold* in crabmeat, cover, and cook on low for 2 hours, stirring every half hour. Serve warm dip with crackers.

## Tip:

This dip is also delicious served with small pastry puffs.

# Pecan-Topped Sweet Potatoes

*Southern-grown pecans add a delicate crunch to sweet potatoes.*

**Preheat oven to 350° Fahrenheit.**

## Ingredients:

cooked and mashed sweet potatoes, enough to make at least 3 cups when mashed
(To cook potatoes, see "Tip.")
¼ cup white sugar
1 teaspoon vanilla
½ cup butter

**topping:**
1 cup brown sugar
⅓ cup plus 2 tablespoons flour
⅓ cup butter
1 cup chopped pecans

*Cooking utensils you'll need:*
*measuring cups*
*measuring spoons*
*cheese shredder*
*slow cooker*
*1 large mixing bowl*
*2 small mixing bowls*
*electric mixer*

## Directions:

Grease baking dish with a small amount of butter and set aside. Use electric mixer to beat potatoes, white sugar, vanilla, and ½ cup butter until smooth. Pour into prepared baking dish and smooth the surface. Mix brown sugar with ⅓ cup flour, and *cut* in butter. In a separate bowl, *toss* pecans with remaining 2 tablespoons flour, then use a fork to mix them into butter mixture, sprinkle over sweet potatoes and bake for 30 minutes.

## Tip:

To cook sweet potatoes, put water in a saucepan, peel and cut the potatoes into chunks and immediately place them in the water, bring to boil over medium heat, cover, lower heat, and simmer until potatoes are tender (about 25 minutes).

## Southern Food History

Pecans grow in all of the Southern states. George Washington, the first president of the United States, enjoyed eating pecans so much that he often carried them in his pocket for easy munching throughout the day. Thomas Jefferson, an avid gardener as well as the third president, planted pecan trees at Monticello, his now-famous home in Virginia. He also gave several pecan trees to Washington in 1775. Some of these trees that were planted at Mount Vernon, Washington's home, still survive. A slave from Louisiana is credited with developing the first grafted pecan tree in the middle of the nineteenth century, thus improving the plant for commercial use. The slave, whose name was Antoine, created "Centennial," a famous type of pecan that later spawned hundreds of new varieties.

## Southern Food History

Is it purloo—or perloo? Or pilau, perlau, plaw, pilaw, or even pilaf? No one agrees on how to spell it or even on how to say it. However you say it and however you spell it, the word comes from Turkish and Persian roots—and it means a stew made from rice and meat. The original dish was first brought to England in the seventeenth century, and became popular as the British Empire spread through the Middle East and into India. In the Southern America colonies, the popularity of rice and the influence of the spice trade made the dish take hold as a traditional favorite.

Southern author Marjorie Kinnan Rawlings wrote, "No Florida church supper, no large rural gathering, is without [purloo]. It is blessed among dishes for such a purpose, or for a large family, for meat goes farther in pilau than prepared any other way." There are a number of variations from region to region, all with different ingredients complementing the rice. From chicken and meat to seafood or vegetables, it's a dish of many possibilities.

# Purloo

*Serve this versatile Southern food as a main dish or side dish.*

## Ingredients:

*3 cups cooked rice (Cook according to package directions.)*
*3 slices bacon*
*1 medium onion, chopped*
*1 medium bell pepper, chopped*
*1 cup thinly sliced okra*
*1 garlic clove*
*1 cup cooked ham, **julienned** (about 3 ounces)*
*1 medium tomato, **seeded** and chopped*
*1 teaspoon thyme*
*½ teaspoon basil*
*⅛ teaspoon red pepper flakes*
*½ teaspoon salt*

*Cooking utensils you'll need:*
*measuring cup*
*measuring spoons*
*large skillet*
*garlic press (optional)*

## Directions:

Cut bacon into pieces, place it in skillet over medium heat, cook until browned, and drain and discard fat. Add onion, pepper, and okra. Use the garlic press to squeeze garlic over the vegetables (or chop it fine). Cook and stir until onion is tender (about 2 or 3 minutes). Stir in ham and cook an additional 3 minutes. Stir in cooked rice and remaining ingredients and heat through, stirring occasionally.

# Red Rice

*This now-famous Southern specialty was first made in South Carolina.*

## Ingredients:

5 slices bacon
¾ cup chopped onion
2 cups cooked rice (Cook according to package directions.)
2 cups canned tomatoes
½ teaspoon salt
½ teaspoon pepper
½ teaspoon hot sauce (optional)

*Cooking utensils you'll need:*
*measuring cups*
*measuring spoon*
*skillet*

## Directions:

Fry bacon until crispy, crumble it, and set it aside. Fry onion gently in bacon fat until translucent. Stir bacon back into skillet. Stir in remaining ingredients and simmer for 40 minutes, adding a little water each time it gets too dry.

## Southern History

Charleston, South Carolina, was established on a natural harbor and experienced successful trade with the West Indies. Pirates, including the infamous Black Beard, also inhabited coastal waters. In 1861, Fort Sumter, located in the harbor and under federal control, was the sight of the first battle of the Civil War when it was fired upon by South Carolina troops.

## Southern History and Tradition

In 1733, James Oglethorpe, a rich idealistic philanthropist from England, sailed up the Savannah River and settled Savannah, the first town in Georgia. His plans to build a virtuous society did not survive the onslaught of slavery and other pressures—but a distinctive Southern culture did evolve.

For instance, in the Deep South, many men are addressed as "Bubba," a corruption of the word "brother." Women are often called "Sister" instead of their given names: Sister Butler, Sister Scott, etc. Younger folk usually address women with whom they are somewhat familiar as "Mis'": Mis' Mary Louise, for example, or Mis' Betty Jane. (Many Southern women have two first names.) As a matter of course, young people address their elders as "sir" and "ma'am."

# Lobster Savannah

## Ingredients:

4 lobsters
1 cup butter
1 small onion, **diced**
1 green bell pepper, diced
½ pound button mushrooms, sliced
¼ cup flour
2 cups light cream (half and half)
2 tablespoons chopped pimento
salt
white pepper
½ cup cooking sherry
1 cup shredded cheddar cheese

Cooking utensils you'll need:
stock pot
measuring cups
measuring spoon
cheese shredder
large skillet
saucepan
broiler pan

## Directions:

Fill stock pot ¾ full of water, place it over high heat, bring to rolling boil, add lobsters, cook until shells turn orange, and remove from heat. When cool enough to handle, remove meat from shells cutting the bottoms of the lobsters and being careful to keep the shells as intact as possible. Break meat into bite-sized pieces. Melt butter in skillet over medium heat, add onion and pepper and cook until tender, stirring occasionally. Stir in mushrooms and flour. Meanwhile, heat light cream in saucepan. Gradually stir heated cream into vegetable mixture. Continue heating and stirring until smooth and add pimento. Salt and pepper to taste, stir in lobster and sherry, and heat through. Spoon mixture into lobster shells and place in broiler pan, top with cheese, and broil until cheese is melted and lobster begins to brown.

# Chicken 'n' Dumplin' Stew

*Add a crisp salad to make this Southern comfort food a complete meal.*

## Ingredients:

1 chicken
2 cups self–rising flour
1 teaspoon salt
3 tablespoons shortening
¼ cup buttermilk

*Cooking utensils you'll need:*
*measuring cups*
*measuring spoons*
*stock pot*
*mixing bowl*
*pastry blender or fork*
*breadboard or other flat surface*
*rolling pin*

## Directions:

Wash chicken (inside and outside) in cold water, place it in the stock pot, cover with cold water, add ½ teaspoon salt, bring to boil, cover, lower heat, and *simmer* for about 2 hours. Remove cooked chicken from pot. When cool enough to handle, remove meat from bones. Discard bones and chicken skin. Skim off any fat that rises to the surface of the chicken stock and discard. Return meat to chicken stock and return to boil. While it is coming to a boil, mix flour and remaining ½ teaspoon of salt in mixing bowl. *Cut* in shortening thoroughly. Cut in buttermilk. Sprinkle breadboard with flour and *knead* dough 5 or 6 times. Roll dough as thin as you can get it, cut it into strips, drop them into the boiling chicken stock, *simmer* for about 10 minutes, and serve.

## Southern Food History

Dumplings are small balls of dough, cooked with meat, vegetables, or fruit. They play a roll in almost every cuisine. For example, Italian cooks make small dumplings, called *gnocchi*; in Germany they make *serviettenknödel*, a tiny light dumpling that usually accompanies pot roasts; and in western Austria they make *kasnocken*, a dumpling made with dry bread and flavored with cheeses. Dumplings are also a large part of Chinese cuisine, where they're usually referred to as *dim sum* and can be steamed, boiled, or fried. True Southern dumplings, however, have a light, fluffy, texture that compliments the chicken stew in which they're cooked. They're a traditional Sunday dinner in many homes.

# Frogmore Stew

*This forty-year-old recipe is a relatively new tradition in the South Carolina Low Country*

## Ingredients:

1 ½ gallons water
3 tablespoons Old Bay Seasoning
3 tablespoons salt
2 pounds kielbasa (or smoked sausage)
12 ears shucked corn
4 pounds shrimp (washed but not peeled)

*Cooking utensils you'll need:*
*stock pot*
*measuring spoon*

## Directions:

Cut the corncobs into 3- or 4-inch lengths. Place water, salt, and Old Bay Seasoning in stock pot and bring to boil over medium/high heat. Carefully add the sausage and *simmer*, uncovered, for about 5 minutes. Stir in corn. Five minutes later add shrimp. Three minutes later your dinner is ready. Drain and serve.

## Southern Food History

One-pot meals that could be cooked over an open fire have been a favorite method of preparing food since colonial times. This particular recipe may have been created by Richard Gay when he was in the National Guard near Beaufort, South Carolina. Mr. Gay wanted to have a cookout for several other members of the Guard. Using leftovers, he whipped up this tasty meal. The Guardsmen liked it so much that popularity of the dish spread. It's also called Low Country Stew (Frogmore is one of the communities in the Low Country) and Beaufort Boil.

# Hoppin' John

*Rice and beans is about as Southern as you can get. They say it's good luck to eat this dish on New Year's Day, but you'll enjoy it any time of the year.*

## Ingredients:

1 cup dried black-eyed peas
4 cups water
2 teaspoons salt
4 slices bacon
1 medium onion, chopped
1 cup long-grain rice

*Cooking utensils you'll need:*
*measuring cup*
*measuring spoon*
*large saucepan*
*skillet*
*rice cooker (see "Tip")*

## Directions:

Wash beans and remove any small stones or other debris. Place beans, water, and salt in large saucepan over medium heat. Bring to boil and simmer until beans are tender. While it's cooking, fry bacon and onion together in the skillet until bacon is crisp and onion is tender (do not drain off the fat). Place uncooked rice, bacon/onion/fat mixture, black-eyed peas, and 1¾ cups bean cooking liquid into rice cooker. Cook until rice has absorbed liquid.

## Tip:

If you don't have a rice cooker, you can simmer the rice in a heavy, covered saucepan over low heat.

## Southern Food History

There is an old saying that if you "eat poor" on New Year's day, you'll "eat rich" for the remainder of the year. That is probably how it began to be considered good luck to eat Hoppin' John on New Year's Day. A resourceful West African cook may have been the first to make this well-loved food. One legend says his name was John, and the dish was so well liked in the household that every time John made it he was kept busy running back and forth to the kitchen to refill plates. There are other legends regarding the name of this now-traditional recipe, however. One suggests that the black-eyed peas "hop" in the pan during cooking.

We may not know the source of the "Hoppin' John" name, but we do know that rice was introduced to South Carolina in the late 1600s. That variety was called "Madagascar," but by the 1800s Carolina residents were calling it "Carolina Gold." That was a fitting name, because it was actually being used in place of money to purchase goods and services.

# Southern Pecan/Sesame Chicken

*Creative Southern cooks have devised countless ways to cook chicken. The combination of pecans and sesame seeds gives this tender chicken a delicious nutty crunch.*

**Preheat oven to 375° Fahrenheit.**

## Ingredients:

1 frying chicken cut into 8 pieces
1 cup flour
1 teaspoon salt
½ teaspoon pepper
¾ cup buttermilk
12 ounces ground pecans (see "Tips")
⅔ cup sesame seeds
½ teaspoon cayenne pepper (optional)
¼ teaspoon nutmeg

*Cooking utensils you'll need:*
*measuring cups*
*measuring spoons*
*food processor (see "Tips")*
*heavy-duty plastic bag*
*2 large bowls*
*baking dish*

## Directions:

Lightly oil the baking dish and set it aside. Wash the chicken, pat it dry with paper towels, and set it aside. Place flour, ½ teaspoon salt, and pepper in the bag. Place buttermilk in one bowl. Mix ground pecans, sesame seeds, cayenne pepper, nutmeg, and remaining salt in the remaining bowl. Place chicken in the bag and shake to coat the pieces. Roll each piece of chicken in the buttermilk and then in the nut/seed mixture. Place chicken in the baking dish, and bake for about 40 minutes (until chicken's juices run clear).

## Tips:

Grind pecans in a food processor. If you don't have a food processor, use a meat grinder with a coarse blade, or cut nuts in pieces and chop them fine in a blender.

If you would like to reduce the fat and calories in this food, remove the chicken skin before coating the meat and substitute fat-free milk for the buttermilk.

You can also use this recipe to cook pork chops or fish.

### Southern Food History

The rural South of the seventeenth and eighteenth centuries had few cities outside of ports like Savannah and Charleston. Travel was long and difficult, and homesteads and plantations were far apart. As a result, guests were expected to visit for days if not weeks. Not only did they need to rest after their long journeys, but they brought news and entertainment to isolated families. Southern hospitality became legendary.

Chicken and pork were served in every possible fashion. Salted, smoked country hams were boiled and baked and served with beaten biscuits. (See page 22.) Greens were served with cornbread. A favorite dessert was often pecan pie—or ambrosia. (See page 52.) Food drew people together, and became a source of comfort and celebration.

*Savannah, Georgia*

## Southern Food History

The word "pecan" comes from *paccan* or *pakan*, an Algonquin Indian word. It is a short word with a rather long meaning: "all nuts requiring a stone to crack." Many pecan varieties, including the hickory, grow wild in southern North America. These nuts were an important food source for several American Indian tribes. The nuts were eaten in many ways including fresh and added to squash, bean, and corn dishes. They were also ground and used as a thickener for stews and to make *pow-cohicora*. This "hickory milk" was made by mixing ground nuts with boiling water.

# *Easy Pecan Praline Strips*

*Preheat oven to 350° Fahrenheit.*

## *Ingredients:*

24 graham crackers
1 cup butter
1 cup brown sugar, packed
1 teaspoon vanilla
1 cup chopped pecans

## *Directions:*

Place the crackers in a single layer in the jelly roll pan. Melt butter in saucepan over low heat. Stir in the brown sugar, increase heat, *simmer* 3 minutes, and stir in vanilla and pecans. Use a tablespoon to gently pour the mixture over crackers, and bake for 10 minutes. Cut crackers, remove them from the pan, and cool before serving.

# Florida Ambrosia

## Ingredients:

¼ cup sugar
1 tablespoon cornstarch
1 cup orange juice
1 teaspoon orange **zest**
2 teaspoons lemon juice
3 oranges, peeled, **seeded**, and sliced (see "Tip")
2 grapefruits, peeled, seeded, and sliced
1 cup halved seedless grapes (either red or green)

*Cooking utensils you'll need:*
*measuring cups*
*measuring spoons*
*saucepan*
*mixing bowl*
*plastic wrap*

## Directions:

Mix sugar and cornstarch in saucepan, stir in orange juice and zest, place over medium heat, and simmer, stirring constantly, until thick and bubbly. Stir in lemon juice, remove from heat, cover, and cool to room temperature. While it is cooling, place prepared fruit in bowl. ***Fold*** cooled sauce into fruit mixture, cover with plastic wrap, and chill. Serve over angel food cake.

## Tip:

With a little practice, you will be able to slice and separate orange and grapefruit sections perfectly. Here's how: Peel fruit with a knife, cutting off all of the pulp. Set the fruit down on a cutting board and hold it carefully with your left hand (if you are right-handed). With your right hand, slide a sharp knife down along the left side of one fruit section (just to the right of the membrane). Then slide the knife up along the right side of the section (just to the left of the membrane), and lift out a perfect fruit section with the membrane left behind. Continue around the fruit until all sections have been cut.

## *Southern Food History*

Although Florida is second only to Brazil in orange production today, the fruit is not native to America. No one knows for sure where oranges originated, but they are thought to have first appeared in India or Southeast Asia. Historians think Ponce de Leon planted the first orange trees in the New World somewhere near St. Augustine, Florida, in the sixteenth century. Between the Civil War and World War I, railroad lines began to be constructed throughout the state. This facilitated the shipment of oranges. Soon it became possible to ship fresh citrus fruit to northern cities such as Baltimore and even New York. Today, Florida produces over one and a half billion gallons of orange juice annually, and more than a hundred thousand people are employed by Florida's orange industry. Incidentally, the world's largest glass of orange juice was created by the American Cancer Society and the Florida Department of Citrus in 1998. The 730 gallons of o.j. weighed in at 8,000 pounds and was contained within a glass that was 8½-feet tall and 5-feet wide.

# Peanut Pie

*Preheat oven to 350° Fahrenheit.*

## Ingredients:

*1 purchased pie crust*
*3 eggs*
*¾ cup brown sugar, packed*
*1 cup light corn syrup*
*1 teaspoon vanilla*
*1½ tablespoons butter, melted*
*¾ cup finely ground peanuts*
*½ cup heavy cream (whipping cream)*
*1 tablespoon confectioner's sugar (powdered sugar)*

*Cooking utensils you'll need:*
*food processor or blender*
*measuring cups*
*measuring spoons*
*mixing bowl*
*electric mixer*

## Directions:

Grind peanuts in food processor or blender and set them aside. Beat eggs, brown sugar, corn syrup, and ¾ teaspoon of the vanilla with electric mixer until well blended. Stir in butter and peanuts, pour into pie crust and bake for about 40 to 45 minutes (until lightly browned and *set*). While pie is still warm, whip cream with confectioner's sugar and remaining ¼ teaspoon of vanilla. Serve each slice of warm pie with a *dollop* of cream.

## Tips:

The cream should be soft and fluffy, but be careful to not overwhip because some whipping cream can quickly become buttermilk with little chunks of butter floating in it. To whip cream faster, chill beaters and the mixing bowl before use.

Here's how to make your own sweet pie crust. Sift 2 cups flour, 2 tablespoons sugar, and 1 teaspoon salt into a bowl. *Cut* in ⅓ cup shortening and ⅓ cup butter. Use a fork to mix in ⅓ cup cold water. (Add more water, 1 tablespoon at a time, if necessary.) Roll dough into a ball. Sprinkle rolling pin and breadboard or other flat surface with flour, and roll dough from the center toward the outside edges, working your way around the ball. Add more flour under edges and to rolling pin as needed. Fold rolled dough in half, set pie plate next to dough, slide dough into plate, open dough up, smooth it into the plate, and crimp the edges as desired.

## Southern Food History and Tradition

More peanuts are grown in Georgia than any other state, so many, in fact, that Georgia is sometimes called "the Goober State." In the African Congo, peanuts were called *nguba*, which is probably the origin of the word "goober."

In the South, echoes of African culture still linger, especially in the Low Country of South Carolina, where the Gullah culture traces its roots to the first slaves that arrived in South Carolina in the early seventeenth century. These original African immigrants were the primary builders of the lucrative rice trade of early colonial America. The skills they used to develop a flourishing culture in Sierra Leone and other Western African countries gave them the know-how to adapt to the swampy marshlands of coastal South Carolina.

In these modern Gullah communities, traditional speech, cooking, and crafts continue to endure. The sweetgrass basket is a thousand-year-old art form that Gullah basket ladies still make and sell. The Gullah dialect is a manner of speaking that is part Elizabethan English and part African. It's spoken with a fast rhythm that makes it difficult for outsiders to understand.

## Southern Food Tradition

The peanut has a long history (it's been found in Peruvian mummy tombs), but peanut butter is a relatively young food. In 1890, Dr. John Kellogg (of corn flakes fame), created peanut butter as a healthy protein substitute that was easy to digest for his patients without teeth. In 1904, peanut butter was promoted as a health food at the St. Louis Universal Exposition. A few years later, agricultural scientist Dr. George Washington Carver developed an improved version of the butter, which attracted even more fans.

Today, more than half the American peanut crop goes into the making of peanut butter. In 1992, Americans consumed 857 million pounds of peanut butter. That's 3.36 pounds per person.

# Peanut Butter Sauce

## Ingredients:

¾ cup milk
1 cup sugar
¼ teaspoon salt
1 tablespoon white corn syrup
6 tablespoons peanut butter
½ teaspoon vanilla

*Cooking utensils you'll need:*
*measuring cups*
*measuring spoons*
*saucepan*

## Directions:

Stir together milk, sugar, and salt in saucepan. Stir in syrup, place over low heat, and cook, stirring constantly, until thick. Stir in peanut butter and vanilla, remove from heat, and cool. Serve over vanilla or chocolate ice cream.

# Peaches & Cream Pie

## Ingredients:

1 baked pie shell
¾ cup sugar
3 tablespoons cornstarch
2 tablespoons flour
¼ teaspoon salt
2 cups milk
2 egg yolks
1 tablespoon butter
1 teaspoon lemon juice
2 cups sliced fresh or canned peaches
½ pint heavy cream (whipping cream)
1 tablespoon confectioner's sugar (powdered sugar)

*Cooking utensils you'll need:*
*measuring cups*
*measuring spoons*
*double boiler*
*wire whisk (optional)*
*mixing bowl*
*electric mixer*

## Directions:

Put water into bottom of double boiler and bring it to a gentle boil over medium heat. Stir together sugar, cornstarch, flour, and salt in the top of double boiler. Slowly stir in milk and place over boiling water. Cook, stirring often, until mixture becomes thicker. While it is cooking, *whisk* egg yolks until well beaten, and slowly add them to the milk mixture. Stir in butter and continue to cook, stirring often, until mixture has thickened. Stir in lemon juice, remove from hot water, and cool. Place 1 cup of the peaches in the baked pie shell, pour filling over peaches, arrange remaining peaches on top, and chill in refrigerator. Whip cream with confectioner's sugar (see "Tips" on page 57) and spread over pie just before serving.

## Southern Food History

The South—especially Georgia—is famous for its peaches, but this fruit actually originated in China, where it was cultivated since the early days of Chinese culture. The Persians brought the peach from China and passed it on to the Romans, who spread it throughout the Mediterranean region. The peach was then brought to America by Spanish explorers in the sixteenth century and eventually made it to England and France in the seventeenth century, where it was a popular although rare treat. American Indian tribes are credited with migrating the peach tree across the United States, taking seeds along with them and planting as they roved the country.

Thomas Jefferson had peach trees at Monticello, but United States farmers did not begin commercial production until the nineteenth century in Maryland, Delaware, Georgia, and finally Virginia. Today, the Southern states lead in commercial production of peaches, but the fruit is also grown in California, Michigan, and Colorado. Peaches are the second largest commercial fruit crop in the United States, second only to apples.

## Southern Food History

Limes were first grown in Southeast Asia. From there, early explorers brought them to the Mediterranean, and Christopher Columbus introduced them to the West Indies. A recipe similar to that for Key lime pie may have made its way to the Florida Keys with settlers from the Bahamas, but they used a fruit called the sour orange to make their dessert. Eventually, Key limes were substituted for the sour orange juice. Sweetened condensed milk was added to the recipe sometime after its invention in 1859. This milk became popular in the Florida Keys, where regular milk was difficult to come by, since the Florida Keys, a group of islands, were isolated from the mainland until they were connected by railroad in 1912.

You can make your pie with Key limes or the more common Persian limes. Most limes available in supermarkets today are the second variety. While many people in the Florida Keys have Key lime trees growing in their yards, Persian limes are the variety produced by most commercial growers. That's because many of the original Key lime groves were destroyed by a hurricane in 1926. Since Persian limes are easier to grow and pick, they were planted to replace many of the lost trees.

# Key Lime Pie

*This dessert has been a tradition in the Florida Keys for a century.*

*Preheat oven to 350° Fahrenheit.*

## Ingredients:

*1⅓ cups graham crackers crumbs (see "Tips)*
*¼ cup plus 6 tablespoons sugar*
*1 tablespoon plus 2 teaspoons butter, melted*
*4 eggs, separated (see "Tips")*
*½ teaspoon cream of tartar*
*1 can sweetened condensed milk*
*½ cup lime juice*

*Cooking utensils you'll need:*
*measuring cups*
*measuring spoons*
*9-inch pie plate*
*electric mixer*
*mixing bowl*

## Directions:

Mix cracker crumbs, ¼ cup of the sugar, and melted butter in pie plate, press firmly into plate, and bake for 8 minutes. Remove from oven and turn temperature down to 250° Fahrenheit. Beat egg whites with cream of tartar, slowly adding remaining 6 tablespoons of sugar, until stiff peaks form, and set it aside. Beat egg yolks well. Stir in sweetened condensed milk and lime juice. Pour lime mixture into graham cracker crust, top with beaten egg whites, and bake until is golden brown.

## Tips:

To turn graham crakers into crumbs, put the crackers in a plastic bag and roll with a rolling pin, until evenly crushed into fine crumbs.

It is best to separate eggs one at a time in 2 small bowls, to be certain no yolk has gotten into the whites, before pouring them into the mixing bowl. If even a speck of yolk contaminates the whites, they will not beat properly.

# Further Reading

Edge, John T. *Southern Belly: The Ultimate Food Lover's Guide to the South.* Athens, Ga.: Hill Street Press, 2002.

Fowler, Damon Lee. *Beans, Greens, and Sweet Georgia Peaches: The Southern Way of Cooking Fruits and Vegetables.* New York: Broadway, 1998.

Glenn, Camille. *The Heritage of Southern Cooking: An Inspired Tour of Southern Cuisine Including Regional Specialties, Heirloom Favorites, and Original Dishes.* New York: Black Dog & Leventhal, 2003.

Gourley, Robbin. *Sugar Pie and Jelly Roll: Sweets from a Southern Kitchen.* New York: Algonquin Books, 2000.

Gunderson, Mary, and Melodie Andrews. *Southern Plantation Cooking (Exploring History Through Simple Recipes).* Mankato, Minn.: Blue Earth Books, 2000.

Hess, Karen. *The Carolina Rice Kitchen: The African Connection.* Columbia: University of South Carolina Press, 1998.

Stamps, Martha Phelps. *The New Southern Basics: Traditional Southern Food for Today.* Nashville, Tenn.: Cumberland House, 2001.

Starr, Kathy. *The Soul of Southern Cooking.* Montgomery, Ala.: NewSouth Books, 2001.

Taylor, Courtney, and Bonnie Carter Travis. *The Southern Cook's Handbook: A Step-by-Step Guide to Old-Fashioned Southern Cooking.* Brandon, Miss.: Quail Ridge Press, 2001.

# *For More Information*

Pecan History
www.vegparadise.com/highestperch.html

Citrus Information
www.ultimatecitrus.com

Food Facts and Lore
www.hungrymonster.com/Foodfacts/Food_Facts.cfm

State Agricultural Profiles
www.agclassroom.org

State History
www.theus50.com

Publisher's note:
The Web sites listed on this page were active at the time of publication. The publisher is not responsible for Web sites that have changed their addresses or discontinued operation since the date of publication. The publisher will review and update the Web sites upon each reprint.

# *Index*

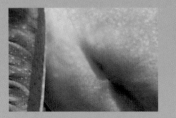

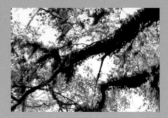

## Author:

In addition to writing, Joyce Libal has worked as an editor for a half dozen magazines, including a brief stint as recipe editor at *Vegetarian Gourmet*. Most of her experience as a cook, however, has been gained as the mother of three children and occasional surrogate mother to several children from different countries and cultures. She is an avid gardener and especially enjoys cooking with fresh herbs and vegetables and with the abundant fresh fruit that her husband grows in the family orchard.

## Recipe Tester / Food Preparer:

Bonni Phelps owns How Sweet It Is Café in Vestal, New York. Her love of cooking and feeding large crowds comes from her grandmothers on both sides whom also took great pleasure in large family gatherings.

## Consultant:

The Culinary Institute of America is considered the world's premier culinary college. It is a private, not-for-profit learning institution, dedicated to providing the world's best culinary education. Its campuses in New York and California provide learning environments that focus on excellence, leadership, professionalism, ethics, and respect for diversity. The institute embodies a passion for food with first-class cooking expertise.

## Recipe Contributor:

Patricia Therrien has worked for several years with Harding House Publishing Service as a researcher and recipe consultant—but she has been experimenting with food and recipes for the past thirty years. Her expertise has enriched the lives of friends and family. Patty lives in western New York State with her family and numerous animals, including several horses, cats, and dogs.

# *Picture Credits*

Corel: cover; PhotoDisc: p. 30; Photos.com: cover, pp. 13, 14, 16, 27, 38, 45, 46, 50, 55, 58, 63, 64, 68; MK Bassett-Harvey: p. 49, Benjamin Stewart: pp. cover, 9, 10, 13, 14, 16, 17, 19, 21, 24, 28, 33, 34, 37, 41, 42, 53, 56, 60, 68, 69, 72.